GETTING A PET

by Harold T. Rober

BUMBA BOOKS™

LERNER PUBLICATIONS ◆ MINNEAPOLIS

Note to Educators:

Throughout this book, you'll find critical thinking questions. These can be used to engage young readers in thinking critically about the topic and in using the text and photos to do so.

Lerner Publications Company
A division of Lerner Publishing Group, Inc.
241 First Avenue North
Minneapolis, MN 55401 USA

For reading levels and more information, look up this title at www.lernerbooks.com.

Library of Congress Cataloging-in-Publication Data

Names: Rober, Harold T., author.
Title: Getting a pet / by Harold T. Rober.
Description: Minneapolis : Lerner Publications, 2017. | Series: Bumba books. Fun firsts | Includes bibliographical
    references and index. | Audience: Ages 4 to 8. | Audience: Grades K to 3.
Identifiers: LCCN 2016022015 (print) | LCCN 2016033372 (ebook) | ISBN 9781512425536 (lb : alk. paper) |
    ISBN 9781512429251 (pb : alk. paper) | ISBN 9781512427493 (eb pdf)
Subjects: LCSH: Pets—Juvenile literature.
Classification: LCC SF416.2 .R63 2017 (print) | LCC SF416.2 (ebook) | DDC 636.088/7—dc23

LC record available at https://lccn.loc.gov/2016022015

Manufactured in the United States of America
1 – VP – 12/31/16

LERNER
SOURCE

Expand learning beyond the printed book. Download free, complementary educational resources for this book from our website, www.lerneresource.com.

Table of Contents

Pets Are Fun

Choosing a pet is fun!

Which pet will

you choose?

Each animal is different.

A fish swims.

A rabbit hops.

People can train pets.

Dogs can be trained to stay

in place.

Pets can learn tricks too.

What are some ways you could train your pet?

Some pets play a lot.

A cat plays with cat toys.

Pets need to stay clean.

Dogs need

to be shampooed.

Pets with long hair should

be brushed.

Hamsters and guinea pigs

have cages.

They need bedding in their cages.

The cages should be cleaned often.

Why do you think you need to clean your pet's cage?

All pets need food

and water.

Iguanas need to eat

every day.

Pets need safe homes.

Make sure cords are out of reach.

Put away anything that could hurt a pet.

Why do you think it is important to keep your pet's home safe?

A new pet can be a great friend.

It will be a member of the family!

Pet Duties

Each kind of pet comes with different duties. Here are some things you will need to do if you get a dog.

- Walk your dog.

- Feed your dog.

- Shampoo your dog's hair.

- Brush your dog's hair.

- Brush your dog's teeth.

- Make sure your dog has fresh water to drink.

Picture Glossary

bedding

a layer of wood chips or paper that goes on the bottom of a cage

cages

containers that some pets are kept in to keep them safe

train

to teach an animal to do something

tricks

clever skills that are learned

Index

Read More

Fortuna, Lois. *Caring for a Pet.* New York: Gareth Stevens Publishing, 2016.

Heos, Bridget. *Do You Really Want a Snake?* Mankato, MN: Amicus Illustrated, 2016.

Kenan, Tessa. *I Love Dogs.* Minneapolis: Lerner Publications, 2017.

Photo Credits